Who Is
Jimmy Carter?

by David Stabler

illustrated by Tim Foley

Penguin Workshop

For Cate & Brian—TF

PENGUIN WORKSHOP
An imprint of Penguin Random House LLC, New York

First published in the United States of America by Penguin Workshop,
an imprint of Penguin Random House LLC, New York, 2022

Visit us online at penguinrandomhouse.com.

Library of Congress Cataloging-in-Publication Data is available.

Printed in the United States of America

ISBN 9780593387382 (paperback)   10 9 8 7 6 5 4 3 2 1 WOR
ISBN 9780593387399 (library binding)   10 9 8 7 6 5 4 3 2 1 WOR

Contents

Who Is Jimmy Carter?

Peanuts. At first, that's all America knew about Jimmy Carter. He was the peanut farmer from Georgia who was running for president of the United States in 1976. And since Americans had not elected a person from the southeastern United States to the White House since Virginian Woodrow Wilson in 1916, he wasn't given much of a chance.

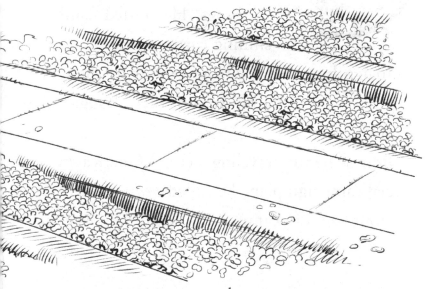

In fact, Jimmy Carter was so unknown outside of Georgia, he had to introduce himself to people at his own campaign stops. "Hello, I'm Jimmy Carter, and I'm running for president," he would say, and flash his wide grin.

Besides peanuts, the one other thing that stood out about Jimmy Carter was his smile. It quickly became the second thing people recognized about the former Georgia governor. Before long, Jimmy got the idea to combine the two things. He started using a smiling cartoon peanut as his campaign logo. Now, whenever anyone thought of peanuts or really big smiles, they thought of Jimmy Carter.

Jimmy began traveling across America in a special campaign plane he called *Peanut One*. He gave out bags of peanuts with his smiling face on the front. People liked his down-home image. They sensed he was a regular person, like them, and not just another politician. More importantly, they began paying attention to him.

The more they listened, the more they liked what he had to say. They learned that Jimmy Carter was more than just a peanut farmer. He was a nuclear engineer, a navy veteran, and a leader in his church. He had been a popular governor of Georgia who favored civil rights for Black Americans. He was known for being honest and straightforward with people—and he had a plan to lead the country.

Slowly but surely, Jimmy won over those who said he could never be elected. Now, when people asked "Who is Jimmy Carter?" the answer was simple: possibly the next president of the United States.

CHAPTER 1
Farm Boy

Home to many tiny family farms, southern Georgia has always been one of the poorest parts of the state. But the small town of Plains—population six hundred—was booming in 1924. That was the year James Earl Carter Jr. (who would be called Jimmy) was born, in the hospital where his mother worked as a nurse. Jimmy's father ran the town's general store.

When Jimmy was four years old, his family left Plains and moved to the nearby town of Archery. There his father, James Earl Carter (who went by his middle name), owned a small farm where he grew cotton, peanuts, and sugarcane. Earl and his wife, Lillian, eventually had three more children: Gloria, Ruth, and William (called Billy). While Earl was a successful farmer, the Carters were not a wealthy family by any means. They had

to pump their own water from a well, had no electricity, and had to go outside to use the bathroom. The open-air "privy" was just a hole cut into a plank of wood. For toilet paper, they used old newspapers.

Farmwork kept Jimmy busy from sunup to sundown. Every day, his father paid him twenty-five cents to feed the hogs, trim the watermelon plants, and "mop the cotton"—an especially

disgusting job in which he smeared the cotton plants with a gooey bug-killing potion made from arsenic (a type of poison), molasses, and water. This homemade insecticide was so sweet-smelling that it attracted swarms of flies and honeybees, which followed Jimmy up and down the rows of cotton. By the end of a long day in the fields, Jimmy's pants were so damp with poison that they actually stood up by themselves when he took them off.

As tough as farmwork was, Jimmy liked the money he made doing it. When he was five, he hit upon his own scheme for putting a few extra coins in his pocket. Peanuts grew in abundance on his father's farm. Boiled peanuts were a popular snack in downtown Plains. In the afternoons, after his chores were done, Jimmy would head out into the field dragging an empty wagon behind him. He would pull handfuls of peanuts out of the ground, load them into the wagon, and take them back to the yard to wash and soak them in salted water. The next morning, he would get up extra early, boil the peanuts, and pack them into tiny bags. He took them into town and sold them for a nickel a bag. In this way, Jimmy learned the value

of hard work—and the importance of peanuts. They were two lessons he would never forget.

Life was not all farmwork for Jimmy. In elementary school, he was known as an obedient, well-behaved, and hardworking student. In the third grade, he won a class prize for reading the most books. He attended Sunday school every weekend, memorized Bible verses, and attended church services regularly. However, he got into his share of mischief as well. He once convinced his sister Gloria to bury a nickel in the ground, telling her it would grow into a money tree. When she wasn't looking, Jimmy dug up the nickel and pocketed it for himself. Another time, Jimmy and his friends hitched one of the family billy goats, Old Gene Talmadge (named after the governor of Georgia), to a go-cart and made him pull them around the yard. On another occasion, Jimmy tried to ride the goat like a bronco, and they both ran head-on into a barbed-wire fence.

When he wasn't working, going to school, or getting into trouble, Jimmy spent much of his time outdoors. He loved to go possum hunting with his father. He became known as one of the best tree-climbers in the town of Archery. His favorite thing to do, though, was collect arrowheads.

There were thousands of them in the woods around Archery, left behind by the Native Americans who had once lived in this part of Georgia.

On rainy days when they could not work in the fields, or in winter when the fields were plowed up, Jimmy and his father would hike the land, gathering up the arrowheads. Sometimes they competed with each other to see who could find the most interesting ones. Eventually, Jimmy had a collection of about two thousand "points," as he called them, which he always kept. It was a fun hobby, but also a reminder of how much Georgia had changed over the years since Native Americans had lived on this land.

As Jimmy would soon learn, there was another group of Americans who also had strong ties to this part of the country, and who would one day change the face of Georgia—and the nation—for the better.

CHAPTER 2
The Old South

In 1929, when Jimmy was five, the US economy collapsed. It was a time that came to be known as the Great Depression. Banks were forced to close. Many stores went out of business. The population of Plains shrank from six hundred to just three hundred people. Before long, out-of-work men—often called tramps— began showing up at the Carters' door. They were looking for something to eat in exchange for doing farmwork. They had heard that Jimmy's mother was a kind woman who did not turn away strangers.

The Great Depression lasted for more than ten years. Things began to improve a bit in 1933 when a new president, Franklin D. Roosevelt,

Franklin D. Roosevelt

offered his "New Deal" plan to improve the economy. Jimmy's father even worked on one of the New Deal projects, helping to bring electricity to rural towns like Plains and Archery. While the terrible economic depression did not affect the Carters as much as some of their neighbors, it did hit one community especially hard.

The town of Archery, where the Carters settled, was home to many African American families. In fact, all of Jimmy's childhood friends were Black, including his best friends Alonzo Davis (called A.D.) and Edmund Hollis. Even though they played together almost every day, A.D. and Edmund were not treated the same as Jimmy was. They were treated worse.

Before the Civil War, Blacks in the South were held as slaves. After the Civil War ended slavery in 1865, they were treated as second-class citizens.

Under the system of segregation—also called "Jim Crow"—Black people were separated from white people by law. Black Americans were not allowed to eat in the same restaurants, drink from the same water fountains, or go to the same schools as white Americans. The facilities reserved for Black people were never as nice as those used by whites. For a community already struggling to survive under the laws of Jim Crow, the Great Depression was a terrible blow.

In time, a civil rights movement rose up to challenge the Jim Crow system. Leaders like Rosa Parks and Dr. Martin Luther King Jr. worked hard to replace the "Old South" with a "New South" of fairness and equality. But when Jimmy was a boy, Black residents who had lived in Archery all their lives were still suffering under the Old South system of segregation. When Jimmy and A.D. went to the movies together, A.D. had to buy his ticket at a different window and sit way up in the third-floor balcony, while Jimmy got to sit in a much better seat right in front of the screen.

Most white people in the South—including Jimmy's father—accepted segregation laws and did not challenge them. Others, like Jimmy's mother, Lillian, did not approve of them. She encouraged Jimmy to make friends with Black children and often invited them into the Carter home to eat in her kitchen.

Jimmy did not understand the need to separate Black people and white people. When he asked, he was simply told that this was the way it had always been. But he could not see why. Because his mother was often out of the house working as a nurse, he and his sisters were left in the care of an elderly Black woman named Rachel Clark. Jimmy came to see her as his second mother. Yet Rachel Clark's home was not as nice as the Carters'. Even though her husband was a supervisor on Earl Carter's farm, he still had to watch what he said around white people. He did not have the same freedoms that they did.

The pastor of Archery's Black Methodist church, Bishop William Decker Johnson, was one of the most respected men in town. Yet when he visited the Carter farm, he had to wait outside in his car and honk the horn, because Jimmy's father would not allow him inside the house. Nevertheless, when Bishop Johnson died in 1936, Lillian Carter took Jimmy to attend his funeral. They were two of the few white people in the church. As Jimmy looked around at the throngs of Black people celebrating Bishop Johnson's life, he began to think that the Old South way of doing things—and his father's acceptance of it—might not be the right way after all.

Lillian Carter (1898–1983)

Bessie Lillian Gordy Carter was one of the best-loved presidential parents in history. Known to everyone as "Miss Lillian," she worked as a nurse in her hometown of Plains, Georgia. In 1966, at the age of sixty-eight, Lillian joined the Peace Corps. For the next two years, she worked in India, helping to take care of people afflicted by leprosy.

Miss Lillian was known for always speaking her mind. She opposed segregation and supported civil rights for Black Americans. When her son became president, she often expressed her views to reporters and appeared on TV talk shows. Jimmy Carter never had a problem with her outspoken ways. "How could Jimmy ever criticize me?" she once asked. "I'm his momma!"

CHAPTER 3
Love and War

While Jimmy looked up to his parents, his real hero was always his uncle Tom Gordy, Lillian's brother. Tom was a US Navy radioman who served on ships in the Pacific Ocean.

As often as he could, Jimmy sent letters to his uncle, telling him all about his life in Georgia. In return, Tom sent back postcards from all the exciting, faraway ports he visited. Jimmy tacked each one of these onto the wall of his bedroom. At night, he would gaze up at them, imagining that one day he too would sail off to sea—even though he had never so much as seen the ocean.

Jimmy dreamed of becoming a naval officer. To do that, he would have to enroll at the US Naval Academy in Annapolis, Maryland. First, though, he had to graduate from high school. That was the easy part for a good student like Jimmy. In June 1941, Jimmy earned his high school diploma, becoming the first person on his father's side of his family to do so. Now he concentrated on his next goal.

To get into the Naval Academy, Jimmy would need to be recommended by a US Congressman. At the time, that didn't seem very likely. At five feet nine inches tall and 121 pounds, Jimmy was much smaller than the typical navy officer. He also had flat feet, which usually disqualified a person from military service. Jimmy began to worry he would never make it into the academy.

On the afternoon of December 7, 1941, as seventeen-year-old Jimmy listened to the radio at home, a news bulletin announced that Japanese airplanes had attacked the US Navy fleet in Pearl Harbor, Hawaii. America was now at war. A few days later, Jimmy learned that his uncle Tom had been captured by the Japanese. Suddenly, in the space of about a week, everything had changed.

As America prepared to go to war, the navy had a great need for good officers—no matter what their size or how flat their feet were. Jimmy's father spoke to their local congressman,  who assured him that he would recommend Jimmy to Annapolis if he spent a year in college first. Jimmy worked hard in college, and in time he earned his appointment. In June 1943, Jimmy boarded a train bound for Annapolis to begin his studies at the US Naval Academy.

Jimmy spent the next three years studying seamanship, engineering, and navigation. He also learned to speak Spanish. During the summers, he underwent naval combat training aboard old battleships. During that time, three important things happened. First, World War II ended. The United States and its allies triumphed over Germany and Japan. Second, Tom Gordy returned home in 1945. Third, Jimmy met the woman he would marry.

Rosalynn Smith

Rosalynn Smith was a friend of Jimmy's sister Ruth. When she was thirteen, Rosalynn's father became seriously ill. Rosalynn's mother had to take on work as a dressmaker to support the family.

World War II

The Second World War began in September 1939 and ended in August 1945. The United States entered the war in December 1941. The war pitted the Allied forces of the United States, Great Britain,

France, and other allied countries against the Axis led by Germany, Japan, and Italy. In all, more than one hundred million people from thirty countries took part in the fighting. More than seventy-five million people died, including many civilians. More than six million Jews were killed by Nazi Germany and their collaborators in a persecution and extermination campaign that has come to be known as the Holocaust.

In Europe, the war ended with the surrender of Germany on May 8, 1945. Japanese forces surrendered on August 15 of that year, after American planes dropped powerful atomic bombs on the Japanese cities of Hiroshima and Nagasaki.

Just before he died, Rosalynn's father made her promise that she would go to college. Rosalynn worked hard at home and at school, helping to support her mother and achieve her father's dream. She graduated near the top of her class from Plains High School and enrolled at Georgia Southwestern College. She hoped to become an architect, but her life changed the day she went on her first date with Ruth Carter's brother, a young naval officer named Jimmy.

They began dating in the summer of 1945, just as the war was ending. Jimmy liked her so much, he almost immediately asked her to marry him. Rosalynn suggested they wait a year so she could finish her second year of college first. On July 7, 1946, one month after Jimmy graduated from the Naval Academy, they were married in a small ceremony in their hometown of Plains.

The newlyweds didn't have much time for a honeymoon. Now a navy officer, Jimmy was assigned to the battleship USS *Wyoming* in Norfolk, Virginia. Jimmy and Rosalynn set off to begin their new life together. A year later, they had their first child, John William "Jack" Carter. A second son, James Earl Carter III, known as "Chip," followed in 1950, and Donnel Jeffrey Carter was born in 1952.

In the meantime, Jimmy was accepted into the navy's submarine training program. For the next few years, the Carters moved around the country as Jimmy attended submarine school in various ports of call. Jimmy even took classes

Jimmy Carter attending the US Navy's submarine school

in nuclear physics, becoming the engineering officer on one of America's first nuclear-powered submarines. But he never got the chance to ship out, because a phone call from his mother soon called him back home on an even more important mission.

CHAPTER 4
Back to Georgia

One day in early 1953, Miss Lillian called Jimmy with some sad news. Jimmy's father, Earl, had become ill with cancer. He didn't have long to live. Jimmy now faced an important decision. He could continue with his navy career or move back home to run the farm and look after his family. After talking it over with Rosalynn, he decided to return to Plains.

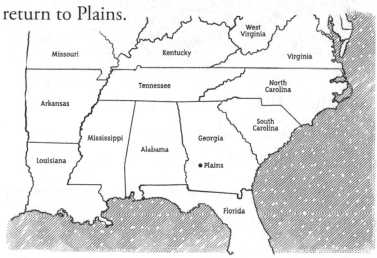

In July 1953, Earl Carter died. With his wife and three children, Jimmy moved back to the family farm. Once settled, he started taking classes to learn as much as he could about growing peanuts and running a business selling farm

supplies. Lillian helped as much as she could, while Rosalynn helped with the bookkeeping. Jimmy's younger brother, Billy, stepped in as well. He taught Jimmy what he knew about the business of running a peanut farm.

In a few short years, Jimmy had the peanut farm thriving and profitable again. He also followed his father and became a leader in the community. He became a deacon at the Baptist church in Plains and began teaching Sunday school, a tradition he would keep up for many years. He also joined the local school board.

Occasionally, Jimmy's views on segregation offended some of the other community leaders. The schools in Plains were still strictly segregated. Black people attended class in one building, white people in another. Jimmy opposed this practice. The churches were also run on the "separate but equal" principle. One year, the white leaders of the Plains Baptist Church voted to ban Blacks from attending Sunday services. Jimmy made his objections known to his fellow deacons, who had all voted for the measure.

In 1958, a group of white residents organized the White Citizens' Council, to support and promote segregation in Plains. Jimmy firmly opposed the group and refused to join.

White Citizens' Council rally

In retaliation, the Council urged its members to boycott Jimmy's business. They refused to buy farm supplies from the Carter family. They hoped to drive Jimmy and his family out of business entirely. The idea of the boycott slowly fizzled out, and the Carter family stayed in business.

Jimmy believed it was time for a change in Plains—and all across Georgia. He felt that the old system of segregating Black and white people should be abolished. He decided that the best way to bring about that change would be to run for office. In 1962, Jimmy ran for a seat in the Georgia state senate. When the results were first announced, it looked like he had lost the election. Then it was discovered that Jimmy's opponent had actually cheated! A new vote was ordered, and Jimmy was declared the winner.

JIMMY
CARTER
FOR STATE
SENATOR

In January 1963, Jimmy headed to Atlanta, the capital of Georgia, to begin working in the state senate. He soon developed a reputation as one of the hardest-working people in state government. He even took a speed-reading course so he could keep up with all the new laws being passed. One of Jimmy's signature causes was protecting voting rights for Black citizens. He also championed education reforms. In his four years in office, Jimmy accomplished so much that people began urging him to run for governor.

Jimmy was up for the challenge. In 1966, after two consecutive two-year terms in the state senate, he announced that he would run for governor of Georgia. He felt sure that the state was ready for a change. Jimmy ran on a bold promise to end segregation in the Peach State. But most white voters in Georgia were not prepared to take that step. To Jimmy's surprise and disappointment, he lost the Democratic primary election to a segregationist, Lester Maddox. Maddox went on to win the general election and become the next governor of Georgia.

Stung by his defeat, Jimmy returned to Plains. In 1967, he and Rosalynn welcomed their fourth child, daughter Amy, into the world. Jimmy almost immediately began to think about his next campaign. He was determined to try again in 1970, when Maddox would be barred from seeking a second term by Georgia's term-limit law.

For the next four years, Jimmy traveled across the state, giving speeches and meeting with elected officials. He managed to convince many of the white leaders who had opposed him to change their minds in time for the next election. But he didn't discuss segregation as much as he had during his campaign four years earlier.

In 1970, Jimmy's hard work paid off. He was elected governor that November with more than 60 percent of the vote. But his success at the polls came with a price. Many Black Georgians now distrusted Jimmy because he had toned down his message about civil rights. They feared he would govern in the interest of the white citizens of Georgia who had elected him. Over the next four years, Jimmy would have to work doubly hard to earn back their trust.

CHAPTER 5
State House to White House

On January 12, 1971, Jimmy was sworn in as governor of Georgia. In his inaugural address, he declared that "the time for racial discrimination is over." The speech made national headlines. But it was Governor Carter's actions that truly shook things up. In his campaign, Jimmy had promised to hire more Black Americans for jobs in state government. As governor, he kept that promise. The number of Black state employees grew by more than two thousand. Jimmy also took important steps to show that Georgia was changing its attitude about segregation. In 1974, he ordered that a portrait of civil rights leader Dr. Martin Luther King Jr. be hung in the state Capitol. While members of the Ku Klux Klan—

an organization that used violence, murder, and intimidation against Black people, and who opposed civil rights for Black Americans—marched in protest, Jimmy refused to back down to the mob.

In other areas of state government, Jimmy also tried his best to make changes. He directed more money to education. He reorganized government agencies to eliminate wasteful spending. He also worked hard to protect Georgia's environment and to preserve its parks and historic places.

The changes began to have an effect. People began talking more about the New South and how the region was making changes that reflected Jimmy's way of thinking. *Time* magazine put Jimmy on its cover. Some people started wondering if Jimmy might be ready for a higher office.

At first, Jimmy shrugged off suggestions that he run for president. But as the end of his four-year term neared, he began to reconsider. After all, if he could bring this much positive change to a state like Georgia, why couldn't he do the same for the United States? There was just one problem. Outside of the American South, hardly anybody knew who Jimmy was. When Jimmy told his mother that he was thinking about running for president, she replied "President of what?" Clearly, Jimmy had his work cut out for him.

In December 1974, one month before his term as governor expired, Jimmy announced that he was running for president of the United States. The next election was still nearly two years away. Jimmy would have plenty of time to introduce himself to the American people.

Jimmy spent the next year on the road, meeting voters and laying out his plan for America. "I'm Jimmy Carter, and I'm running for president" became his catch phrase. "Jimmy who?" some replied at first. But over many months, people all over the country got to know him.

Jimmy was helped by the fact that many better-known candidates decided not to run in 1976. The current president, Gerald Ford, had been vice president when Richard Nixon resigned following the Watergate scandal.

Gerald Ford and Richard Nixon

Many Americans had come to mistrust the way things were being run in Washington, DC. They were looking for a new candidate who could bring fresh energy to the nation's capital.

When Democrats began selecting their nominee in January 1976, Jimmy was the surprise winner of early contests in Iowa and New Hampshire. Suddenly, the once-unknown candidate vaulted to the top of the pack. His so-called "peanut brigade" of supporters followed him wherever he went. By the time spring

arrived, Jimmy had a large lead over his rivals. In July, Democrats officially nominated him to be their candidate in the November presidential election.

For his vice presidential running mate, Jimmy selected Senator Walter Mondale of Minnesota. Known as "Fritz," Mondale was a seasoned politician whose presence seemed to comfort voters who were still unsure about Jimmy's lack of national experience. "Grits and Fritz," as they were called, made for a strong team. ("Grits" referred to Jimmy's southern upbringing, where grits—a type of porridge made from corn—are often served for breakfast.) Polls showed the two Democrats easily defeating the Republican team of Gerald Ford and Robert Dole.

Over the summer, President Ford mounted a comeback, and was within a few points of Jimmy's lead when the two men met in their second debate on October 6. During the debate, Ford made a huge mistake on a question about foreign policy, while Jimmy gave confident and reassuring answers. Although polls conducted after the exchange showed Jimmy widening his

lead, the final result was incredibly close. Jimmy Carter was elected president by just 2 percent of the vote.

The campaign was over. The hard work of leading the country was about to begin.

Jimmy Carter and Gerald Ford debate in 1976

Walter Mondale (1928–2021)

Walter Mondale

The grandson of Norwegian immigrants, Walter Mondale first became involved in politics as a college student at the University of Minnesota. He held several important offices, including Minnesota state attorney general, US senator, and vice president under Jimmy Carter.

Mondale was a strong supporter of Carter's policies and believed that he, as the vice president, should be the president's full partner and key advisor on all important decisions. After leaving office, Mondale became the Democratic presidential nominee in 1984. He made history that year when he named New York Congresswoman Geraldine Ferraro his running mate, making her the first female vice presidential candidate in American history.

After he lost his race for president, Mondale became an ambassador to Japan under President Bill Clinton. He ran for the Senate once more time, in 2002, but was narrowly defeated. He retired from public life but continued to speak out on issues that were important to him until his death at age ninety-three.

CHAPTER 6
Mr. President

On January 20, 1977, Jimmy Carter took the oath of office as America's thirty-ninth president. At the inaugural ceremony, Jimmy surprised people by wearing a simple business suit instead of the top hat and tuxedo worn by previous presidents. And there were more surprises in store.

During the inaugural parade, Jimmy shocked everyone by walking from the Capitol building to the White House, arm in arm with his family.

He was the first president to walk, rather than ride, to the White House! The bold move was part of Jimmy's plan to show Americans their new president was a humble "man of the people."

Jimmy and Rosalynn moved into the White House with their nine-year-old daughter, Amy, who was the first child to live in the White House since 1963. She brought along her pet cat, Misty Malarky Ying Yang. Amy became famous for roller-skating in the White House and hosting sleepovers in a tree house on the White House lawn. The other Carter children, who were all grown up, remained in Georgia. Jimmy's outspoken mother, who was called Miss Lillian by just about everyone, stayed at the family farm in Plains but visited the White House often.

The new commander in chief started making decisions immediately. While running for president, Jimmy had promised to pardon those

Amy Carter skates at the White House

who had refused to fight in the Vietnam War. He kept that promise. He delivered on a plan to establish a Department of Energy. And he followed through on his pledge to pressure other countries to respect the human rights of their people. By the end of his first year in office, Jimmy had a high approval rating from the American public.

Jimmy's informal style was also a hit with the American people. They liked that he wore jeans around the White House and served barbecue to guests instead of hosting fancy dinners and serving French food. Miss Lillian and Amy became celebrities in their own right. Even Jimmy's brother, Billy, made the cover of *Newsweek*, promoting his own brand of beer.

If Jimmy's first year in office was largely successful, though, there were rough times ahead. An outsider to the ways of Washington, Jimmy did not always get along with leaders in Congress. His stubbornness cost him the support of members of his own party. And when Jimmy announced a plan to return the Panama Canal to the nation of Panama, most Republicans—and many Democrats—opposed him. (The canal had been built by the United States and managed by both the US and Panama since 1904.) The Panama Canal Treaty did eventually pass—but just barely.

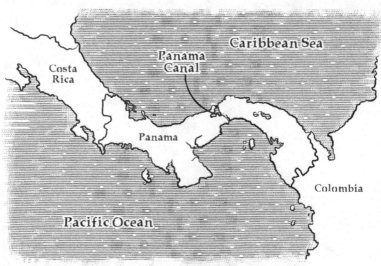

Jimmy also had trouble getting his program for conserving energy through Congress.

In 1978, Jimmy tried another bold move that helped revive his presidency. He invited Menachem Begin and Anwar Sadat, the leaders of Israel and Egypt, to meet with him to see if they could work out a peace treaty between their two countries. After twelve days of meetings

Anwar Sadat, Jimmy Carter, and Menachem Begin

in the Maryland mountains at the presidential retreat called Camp David, the two sides agreed to the Camp David Accords in September 1978 and returned to sign it at the White House the following March. The treaty ended thirty years of war. Jimmy was praised for his role in bringing the two sides together.

The peace treaty between Egypt and Israel was the greatest achievement of Jimmy's presidency. He hoped it would boost his popularity enough that he could get his plan for energy conservation through Congress. But it was not to be. Congress did pass an energy bill, but it was not the one that Jimmy had proposed. Meanwhile, gasoline prices were starting to rise. This led to a slowdown in the economy. More and more Americans were losing their jobs. The price of groceries and other products was climbing higher. As 1978 came to a close, Jimmy watched his popularity drop.

Gas prices rise at the end of 1978

Americans hoped there would be better times ahead. But the next year turned out to be even more difficult—as Jimmy faced his biggest crisis yet.

Camp David

Camp David is the name of the official presidential retreat in Maryland's Catoctin Mountain Park. Originally called Hi-Catoctin, the camp opened in 1939 and became the presidential retreat in 1942. It was renamed Shangri-La by President Franklin D. Roosevelt. In 1953, President Dwight D. Eisenhower renamed it again, calling it Camp David in honor of his grandson David.

Presidents and their families visit Camp David for weekend getaways as well as working vacations. Many foreign leaders have met with the US president there, including Russian president Vladimir Putin and British prime ministers Winston Churchill, Margaret Thatcher, and Tony Blair. President Ronald Reagan made the most trips to Camp David—189 in all—while Harry Truman only visited ten times. The name Camp David will forever be linked to the peace accord signed there between the leaders of Israel and Egypt in 1979.

Aspen Lodge at Camp David

CHAPTER 7
Tough Times

As he entered the third year of his term as president, Jimmy Carter faced more and more challenges. The countries that supplied most of the oil that powered America's cars cut off the supply. As a result, there were long lines at gas stations, and the price of gas was very high.

To make matters worse, Americans were having trouble finding jobs. Many of Jimmy's plans to address these problems were stalled in Congress.

Then, an international crisis turned everyone's attention to the Middle East. The ruler of Iran, Reza Shah Pahlavi, was seriously ill and traveling the world seeking medical treatment. While he was out of the country, a revolution toppled the government. Many in Iran considered the Shah a tyrant. The United States considered him

Mohammad Reza Shah Pahlavi

an important ally, though, and didn't want to be seen as betraying a friend.

On November 4, 1979, a group of angry students stormed the United States embassy in Iran's capital city of Teheran. To make a statement that would get the attention of the US government, they took fifty-two Americans hostage. The Iranian students promised to set them free only if the United States returned the ailing Shah home for punishment. Jimmy refused to bargain with the students. The Iran hostage crisis had begun.

An American is held hostage in Iran

Jimmy and his team worked day and night to get the hostages freed. He even ordered a squad of helicopters to attempt a dangerous rescue mission. But the choppers crashed in the desert and the mission failed. As the hostage takers held fast to their demands, many people began to blame Jimmy for not resolving the ongoing crisis.

Late in 1979, the Soviet Union invaded the small nation of Afghanistan, hoping to install a Communist government there over which they could rule. In response, Jimmy cut off

shipments of grain to the Soviet Union. He also announced that the United States would not take part in the upcoming Olympic Games in Moscow. Jimmy now had two international problems on his hands as he headed into his reelection campaign in 1980.

That year, Jimmy would face not one but two challenges from political rivals. Massachusetts Senator Edward "Ted" Kennedy announced that he would seek the Democratic nomination. He claimed to speak for all Democrats who were disappointed in President Carter's leadership. While Kennedy ran a strong campaign and defeated Jimmy in several primary elections, in the end, he came up short. The Democrats renominated Jimmy for a second term at their convention in July 1980.

Jimmy Carter and Ted Kennedy in 1980

Now Jimmy faced Republican Ronald Reagan in the November general election. A former actor, Reagan ran on a platform of building up the

Ronald Reagan

military and cutting taxes. He claimed that Jimmy had failed to provide strong leadership during the Iran hostage crisis.

Throughout the summer, polls showed the two candidates locked in a close race. Voters liked that Jimmy was experienced and kept a cool head in a crisis. Some worried that Reagan was too quick-tempered and might plunge the United States into a war. Another group of voters liked the third candidate in the race, Congressman John Anderson of Illinois. For a while it looked like it would be a very close election, just as it was in 1976.

John Anderson

That all changed when Jimmy and Ronald Reagan had their only debate in late October 1980. Voters watching on television liked Reagan's easygoing style. Some thought that Jimmy appeared to be too stiff and too serious. "Are you better off now than you were four years ago?" Reagan asked the audience watching at home.

Jimmy Carter and Ronald Reagan debate in 1980

Many voters decided that they were not better off under Jimmy Carter's leadership. Some had lost jobs or watched the price of gas and groceries go higher and higher. Others were disturbed by the Iran hostage crisis. In the end, many people simply decided it was time for a change.

On November 4, 1980, Ronald Reagan defeated Jimmy Carter in a massive landslide. Jimmy won only six states, including his home state of Georgia. It was a terrible blow. Jimmy and Rosalynn were devastated.

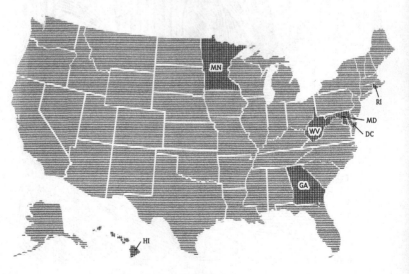

The six states that President Jimmy Carter won in 1980

Despite his sadness over the outcome of the election, Jimmy kept working hard to complete his term as president. He vowed to do everything he could to get the hostages freed from Iran. On January 20, 1981, the day Ronald Reagan was sworn in as America's fortieth president, Jimmy's hard work finally paid off. A deal was announced to set the hostages free after 444 days in captivity. Jimmy was thrilled. Although he would not be present at the White House to see them all return home, he knew in his heart that he had done everything he could to win their freedom. As he packed his things to return to Plains, he could look back with pride at a job well done.

CHAPTER 8
Starting Over

Jimmy Carter was just fifty-six years old when he left office. But he was not ready to retire just yet. With Rosalynn and Amy by his side, he moved back into the family home in Plains, Georgia. There a busy new life awaited them.

Jimmy's first order of business was to see to the peanut farm. It had been maintained but not well cared for in the Carters' absence and had fallen deeply in debt. Ultimately, the Carters decided to sell the farm and the warehouse. Meanwhile, Rosalynn set about sprucing up their home, which no one had lived in for years. Amy enrolled in high school and worked hard to adjust to life away from the White House, with

no bowling alley or swimming pool—or Secret
Service agents—to distract her.

Jimmy began teaching Sunday school again. He set up a wood shop in his garage and helped Rosalynn with repairs around the house. They planted a garden together and learned how to preserve their fruits and vegetables. Sometimes Jimmy went trout fishing.

Every now and then, a world leader would

come to Plains to thank Jimmy for the work he had done as president. The president of Egypt dropped by, as did the prime minister of Israel. So did the ex-president of France and several of the freed hostages who had been held in Iran. Jimmy enjoyed these visits. He began to think more about how he could advance the causes he believed in, even though he was no longer serving the American people as president.

In 1981, Jimmy drew up plans for his presidential library. Most ex-presidents used their library to store their personal letters and important papers. Jimmy had other ideas. He wanted to create a place where students, scholars, and world leaders could come to meet and talk about ways to promote world peace, human rights, and democracy. In 1982, the Carter Presidential Center opened its doors to the public in Atlanta, Georgia. This would be Jimmy's home office for the next forty years.

CARTER PRESIDENTIAL CENTER

When he wasn't at the Carter Center, Jimmy worked on a book about his time as president. Published in 1982, *Keeping Faith* 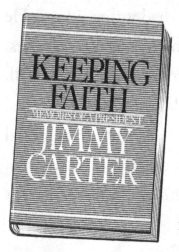 was a huge bestseller. The book detailed all of Jimmy's most important accomplishments, from the Panama Canal Treaty to the Camp David Accords. Even those who had voted for Ronald Reagan in 1980 began to reconsider—and to think more highly of—Jimmy's time in office.

As the 1984 election approached, some members of the Democratic Party began urging Jimmy to run for president again. But Jimmy had a different kind of project in mind. In March of that year, he and Rosalynn volunteered to build houses for the needy with the Georgia-based charity organization called Habitat for Humanity.

News reports showed the former president and first lady hammering nails and patching leaky roofs. They enjoyed the work so much that they led a Habitat for Humanity work group to New York City later that year, creating safe, affordable houses for nineteen families. They called it the Carter Work Project and continued to complete one project each year between 1984 and 2019.

In the 1984 election, Jimmy was proud to endorse his old friend Walter Mondale for president. He spoke on Mondale's behalf at the Democratic Convention, where he received a standing ovation. He was especially pleased that Mondale had invited Geraldine Ferraro to join him on the ticket as his vice presidential running mate, the first woman in that role. But the historic Mondale-Ferraro ticket was not so lucky at the polls. The pair won only one state as Ronald Reagan and his vice president, George H. W. Bush, cruised to reelection.

Walter Mondale and Geraldine Ferraro

In 1989, Bush succeeded Reagan as president and gave Jimmy a challenging new assignment. He asked him to travel to Panama to lead an international effort to make sure the votes in that nation's election were counted correctly. There was suspicion that Panama's dictator, Manuel Noriega, would not conduct the election in a free and fair manner. When Jimmy arrived

Manuel Noriega

in Panama, he could see that those suspicions were correct. After inspecting a number of polling places, he went on television and gave a speech in Spanish informing the citizens of Panama that their votes were not being counted fairly. The Panamanian people, who respected Jimmy from his time as president, listened to what he had to say. Noriega was furious.

A grateful President Bush later sent Jimmy on a similar mission to Nicaragua. Monitoring elections in foreign countries soon became one of Jimmy's specialties. Besides Panama and Nicaragua, Jimmy ventured to the Dominican Republic and Paraguay to oversee their vote counts. When Jimmy could not go himself, he sent a team of experts from the Carter Center.

Jimmy Carter meets Paraguay's newly elected president,
Juan Carlos Wasmosy, in 1993

Peace negotiations also took up a lot of Jimmy's
time. In 1993, President Bill Clinton sent him to
Haiti to persuade that nation's dictator to leave the
country. The next year, Jimmy traveled to North
Korea to try to work out a peace treaty with the
United States. In Bosnia, a nation at war, Jimmy
helped broker a truce. In Sudan, he helped put an
end to twelve years of civil war. How did he do
it? In part by inviting one of the rebel leaders to

attend one of his Sunday school classes in Plains!

Jimmy's role as a global peacemaker earned him many new fans. Henry Kissinger, a former US secretary of state, called him America's "missionary of peace." Rosalynn dubbed Jimmy's overseas work "building hope." Jimmy called it "waging peace." However you describe it, it has undoubtedly made the world a safer place.

Jimmy Carter on one of his many visits to Sudan

CHAPTER 9
A Legacy of Peace

As the twentieth century drew to a close, Jimmy began to reap the rewards of a lifetime of service to his country—and the world. In 1999, President Clinton awarded him the Presidential Medal of Freedom—the highest civilian honor an American citizen can be given. Rosalynn received one, too, making them the first First Couple to get the award at the same time.

Three years later, in 2002, Jimmy learned that he was getting an even higher honor. One morning in Plains, he took a phone call from Oslo, Norway, informing him that he would be awarded the Nobel Peace Prize for his work resolving conflicts as both president and private citizen. He and Rosalynn flew to Oslo to accept the award in person. There they were greeted by a cheering crowd. In his acceptance speech,

Jimmy urged people everywhere "to seek an end to violence and suffering throughout the world."

In the years that followed, Jimmy kept up his active schedule. He toured Cuba in 2002 and again in 2011, becoming the first US president to visit that country since Calvin Coolidge in 1928. He continued to volunteer as a carpenter for Habitat for Humanity. Between 1984 and 2019, Rosalynn and Jimmy Carter personally built or repaired more than four thousand homes!

Jimmy Carter meets with the president of Cuba,
Raúl Castro, in 2011

The Presidential Medal of Freedom

The Presidential Medal of Freedom is an award given by the president of the United States to recognize a person's nonmilitary contribution to American society or the benefit of the world. John F. Kennedy was the first president to give out the award. Barack Obama gave out the most—132 over his eight years in office.

The Medal of Freedom is often awarded to important figures in the arts, entertainment, science, and sports. The first recipient of the Medal of Freedom was Marian Anderson, the pioneering singer who was the first Black person to perform with the New York Metropolitan Opera. Other well-known figures who have earned the award include scientist Stephen Hawking, boxer Muhammad Ali, and talk show host Oprah Winfrey. Seven US presidents have received the Medal of Freedom themselves.

Jimmy kept on writing books, about one or two a year every year until 2015. After completing his memoir, *Keeping Faith*, in 1982,

Jimmy and Rosalynn wrote the book *Everything to Gain* together

Jimmy wrote more than twenty books. Rosalynn Carter wrote four of her own, and they wrote one together. They're not all about politics and world affairs. Jimmy's books include *The Hornet's Nest*, a novel about the American Revolution— the first novel ever written by a US president—as well as a collection of poems called *Always a Reckoning* and a picture book, *The Little Baby Snoogle-Fleejer*, with illustrations by his daughter, Amy.

In August 2015, Jimmy, then ninety years old, announced that he had been diagnosed with cancer. At first, doctors told him that he had just a few weeks to live. By the following March, however, the disease had stopped spreading. Jimmy was declared cancer-free and was able to resume his active lifestyle. But there were more health challenges ahead.

In 2017, Jimmy was building homes in Canada on a hot day when he collapsed from dehydration. He quickly recovered. In May 2019, he had surgery to repair a broken hip after he fell at his home in Plains. A few months later, he fell again and nicked his head on a cabinet. He was taken to a hospital and received fourteen stitches above his eye. He had to wear a bandage over one eye for several weeks until the cut healed.

Through it all, Jimmy kept a positive outlook on life. His strong religious faith helped guide him though all the tough times. On March 22, 2019, Jimmy reached another milestone. At 94 years and 172 days old, he became the oldest living former president ever, passing the previous record held by George H. W. Bush. In 2021, Jimmy and Rosalynn joined ex-presidents Bill Clinton, George W. Bush, Barack Obama, and their wives, the former first ladies, to film a television commercial encouraging Americans to get the COVID-19 vaccine. Even at his advanced age, he was still prepared to answer the nation's call to service.

Jimmy Carter continues to inspire others to a life of service. His strong Christian faith and close family remain his inspiration. Though slowed down by ill health, Jimmy continued to teach his regular Sunday school class well into his nineties. He and Rosalynn celebrated

seventy-five years of marriage in July 2021. They now have twenty-two grandchildren and great-grandchildren. Many of them live near his home in Georgia and visit him as often as they can. Jimmy and Rosalynn still support Habitat for Humanity, even if they don't pick up a hammer quite as often as they once did.

Today, Jimmy Carter is remembered as much for his work outside the White House as for his time in it. "I can't deny I'm a better ex-president

than I was a president," he once said. His work building houses for the needy and speaking out on behalf of democracy, peace, and human rights is as important to him as any bill he signed in the Oval Office. "I have one life and one chance to make it count for something," he told the *New York Times*. "My faith demands that I do whatever I can, wherever I am, whenever I can, for as long as I can with whatever I have to try to make a difference."

Timeline of Jimmy Carter's Life

1924 — Born in Plains, Georgia

1928 — Moves with his family to the town of Archery, Georgia

1941 — Graduates from Plains High School

1946 — Graduates from the US Naval Academy in Annapolis, Maryland

— Marries Rosalynn Smith

1947 — Son Jack is born

1950 — Son James is born

1952 — Son Donnel is born

1962 — Elected to the Georgia state senate

1967 — Daughter Amy is born

1970 — Elected governor of Georgia

1976 — Elected president of the United States

1978 — Brokers the Camp David peace agreement between Israel and Egypt

1981 — Negotiates for the release of hostages held in Iran

1982 — Founds the Carter Presidential Center

1999 — Awarded the Presidential Medal of Freedom

2002 — Awarded the Nobel Peace Prize

2012 — Travels to Haiti with Habitat for Humanity

2021 — Encourages citizens to receive the COVID-19 vaccine

Timeline of the World

1924 — The first Macy's Thanksgiving Day Parade is held in New York City

1932 — Franklin D. Roosevelt is elected president of the United States

1938 — The first Superman comic book, *Action Comics* no. 1, is published

1941 — The United States officially enters World War II after Japan attacks Pearl Harbor naval base in Hawaii

1955 — Disneyland opens in Anaheim, California

1963 — The March on Washington calls for civil rights for Black Americans

1969 — Astronaut Neil Armstrong becomes the first person to walk on the moon

1977 — The first Star Wars film is released

1981 — Sandra Day O'Connor becomes the first woman appointed to the US Supreme Court

2004 — The Boston Red Sox win the World Series for first time since 1918

2009 — Barack Obama is sworn in as the first Black president of the United States

2018 — South Korea hosts the Winter Olympics in PyeongChang

2021 — Perseverance Rover lands on Mars

Bibliography

*Books for young readers

Carter, Jimmy. *Why Not the Best?* Nashville: Broadman Press, 1975.

*Hobkirk, Lori. *James Earl Carter: Our 39th President*.
Chanhassen, MN: The Childs World, 2020.

*Joseph, Paul. *Jimmy Carter*. Edina, MN: ABDO Publishing
Company, 1999.

*Kramer, Barbara. *Jimmy Carter: A Life of Service*. Berkeley
Heights, NJ: Enslow, 2005.

*Lazo, Caroline. *Jimmy Carter: On the Road to Peace*. Parsippany, NJ:
Dillon Press, 1996.

*Rose, Rachel. *Jimmy Carter: President and Humanitarian*.
Minneapolis: Bearport Publishing, 2021.

*Santella, Andrew. *James Earl Carter Jr.: Profiles of the Presidents.*
Minneapolis: Compass Point Books, 2003.

*Stabler, David. *Kid Presidents: True Tales of Childhood from
America's Presidents*. Philadelphia: Quirk Books, 2014.

Zelizer, Julian. *Jimmy Carter*. New York: Henry Holt, 2010.

Made in the USA
Las Vegas, NV
19 May 2024